EAT THIS!

How Fast-Food Marketing Gets You to Buy Junk (and how to fight back)

ANDREA CURTIS

Illustration by **PEGGY COLLINS**

Red Deer Press

For my boys, as ever – A.C.

Text copyright © 2018 Andrea Curtis
Illustrations copyright © 2018 Peggy Collins

Cover (top left, top right, bottom left), pages i, ii, 5, 7, 9, 11, 13, 17, 19, 21, 23, 27, 29, 33 © iStock.com; page 8, by Jamie Robertson, Black Frog Photography; page 14, image courtesy of Sustain, the alliance for better food and farming; cover (bottom right), pages 15, 25 © Shutterstock.com; pages 17, 27 © Graphicstock; page 22, photo courtesy of London Agency; page 35, © Karri North.

Published in Canada by Red Deer Press, 195 Allstate Parkway, Markham, Ontario L3R 4T8

Published in the United States by Red Deer Press, 311 Washington Street, Brighton, Massachusetts 02135

All inquiries should be addressed to Red Deer Press, 195 Allstate Parkway, Markham, Ontario L3R 4T8.

www.reddeerpress.com

10 9 8 7 6 5 4 3 2

Red Deer Press acknowledges with thanks the Canada Council for the Arts, and the Ontario Arts Council for their support of our publishing program. We acknowledge the financial support of the Government of Canada through the Canada Book Fund (CBF) for our publishing activities.

 Canada Council   Conseil des arts
for the Arts   du Canada

 ONTARIO ARTS COUNCIL
CONSEIL DES ARTS DE L'ONTARIO
an Ontario government agency
un organisme du gouvernement de l'Ontario

Library and Archives Canada Cataloguing in Publication

Curtis, Andrea, author
      Eat this! : how fast-food marketing gets you to buy junk (and how to fight back) / Andrea Curtis ; illustrations by Peggy Collins.

Includes bibliographical references.
ISBN 978-0-88995-532-5 (softcover)

      1. Advertising–Food. 2. Junk food–Marketing. 3. Food industry and trade. I. Title.

HF6161.F616C87 2017   659.19'6413   C2017-901600-8

Publisher Cataloguing-in-Publication Data (U.S.)

Names: Curtis, Andrea, author. | Collins, Peggy, 1975-, illustrator.

Title: Eat This! : how fast-food marketing gets you to buy junk (and how to fight back) / Andrea Curtis; illustration by Peggy Collins.

Description: Richmond Hill, Ontario : Red Deer Press, 2017. | Includes bibliographic references. | Summary: "Eat This examines how the fast-food industry uses advertising and marketing to influence children and young adults, while providing means and measures to combat the ubiquitous problem" – Provided by publisher.

Identifiers: ISBN 978-0-88995-532-5 (pbk.)

Subjects: LCSH: Junk food – Health aspects – Juvenile literature. | BISAC: JUVENILE NONFICTION / Health & Daily Living / Diet & Nutrition.

Classification: LCC TX370.C878 | DDC 613.2 – dc23

Edited for the Press by Peter Carver
Cover and Interior Design by Kong Njo

Printed by Sheck Wah Tong Printing Press Ltd., Hong Kong.

Contents

Every day we're bombarded with marketing trying to sell us stuff.

It's on the streets and sports fields, on buses and on TV, radio, the Internet, cell phones—even in our schools.

A lot of these promotions are for food and drinks. Selling food to young people is a huge, worldwide industry. You're an important market! Companies spend billions of dollars a year to encourage you to visit their restaurants and eat or drink their products.

But much of the marketing is for things that aren't healthy. Food like French fries, chips, chocolate bars, cookies, and hamburgers, beverages like soda and sports drinks.

What's more, marketing works. We wear fast-food logos on our T-shirts. We sing their jingles. We send ads to our friends and link to them on social media. Even before kids can read, many know the popular brands by their symbols and characters.

Marketers make eating and drinking these unhealthy foods and beverages sound cool—even fun. One out of every three American children eat fast food every single day.

But the results of eating too much of this kind of food aren't fun at all.

There are serious health risks that come from too much sugar, salt, and fat in your food. Health problems—such as obesity, diabetes, heart disease, and certain types of cancers—that can make you very, very ill. Research published in the journal *Clinical Pediatrics* also suggests that kids who eat a lot of junk food do less well in school.

The environment we live in suffers, as well. Think about all the plastic and paper packaging from fast food and drinks, as

Fast-food restaurants spend nearly five billion dollars a year marketing their products in the U.S. alone.

The Canadian province of Quebec has banned advertising to children since 1980. People in the province buy less junk food and have lower rates of overweight and obesity than the rest of Canada.

well as all the food we simply throw away. Or the vast amount of fuel used to operate the farms and factories that grow, prepare, and process these products all over the world.

With marketing designed to convince you to eat and drink this stuff—even if you know it's not healthy for you or good for the planet—it's hard to know what to think. Scientists say young people are particularly easy to sway with marketing messages because their brains are still developing as they grow and mature.

Some countries have decided it isn't fair to promote unhealthy food and drinks to young people and have made it against the law. Other nations have created rules to limit marketing to children or have allowed companies to make their own guidelines.

But unless you live in a cave, it's impossible to entirely escape the reach of fast-food and drink marketing. That's why kids also need information to understand the way it works.

This guide to fast-food marketing is designed to give you all the tools you need to identify what companies are trying to sell you and how they're doing it. You might be surprised to see how subtle the techniques can be. You might also get inspired by the kids, parents, and organizations all over the world fighting back and telling marketers they're *not* going to eat it up.

About one-third of all the food produced around the world is lost or wasted—that's approximately 1.3 billion tonnes of edible food at a cost of $750 billion dollars every year. Try to imagine the weight of over six million full-scale models of the Statue of Liberty, and you can begin to see how much waste we produce.

What is Marketing?

Marketing is the art and science of persuasion. It is a way of communicating ideas so people will feel what the marketer wants them to feel or buy the product the marketer wants them to buy. Advertising is one of the tools marketers use to get their message out.

Ads have been around for thousands of years. In Roman times, merchants painted them directly on the outside walls of their businesses; in ancient Egypt, special paper called papyrus was used for posters promoting everything from an upcoming festival to a political candidate. Mostly, these early ads focused simply on letting people know the item (or person) was available—and was of the best quality, of course!

Today, marketing is more complicated. When there are so many possible items to buy, it's no longer enough to simply let people know your product exists. Marketers do lots of research to understand people's behavior and buying habits so they can create campaigns that work. Over the years, creative marketers have invented thousands of ways to get people interested in what they are selling—from flashy billboards to handwritten postcards, from newspaper, TV, and web-based ads to signs on the back of public bathroom doors!

Many ads depend on the power of repetition. Psychologists—scientists who study why people behave the way they do—say just seeing a brand over and over can make us want to eat or drink the product. And the younger we are when we start seeing it, the more likely we are to become loyal.

Advertising is a nearly $600 billion global business. That's a lot of money to convince people to spend their money!

Being "media-literate" means understanding the role of media (TV, radio, print, Internet, apps, film, etc.) in the world. When we understand its purpose and meaning, we can make smart, informed decisions about how we respond to the messages we see and hear.

But probably the most powerful part of modern marketing is the way it plays with our emotions. Ads and other marketing tools are designed to appeal to people at different ages and stages. Think about all the ads you've seen in your life. When you were little and your needs were largely love and affection, ads were soft and cuddly. As you've grown older and have more independence, you've had to face up to your fears. That's why ads aimed at older children often feature gross or scary elements. Products for tweens and teenagers—who are trying to figure out who they are and how to fit in—are pitched as an excellent way to make you cool.

But as advertising has taken over our public and private spaces, people have also become more suspicious of what they're being sold. We no longer trust everything we see or read or hear.

Marketers have responded by creating ads and other promotions that don't seem like ads at all. Some are hilarious, smart, or just really interesting. In fact, many people think of advertising as an important part of our culture: entertainment that informs us. Others complain that ads trick us into buying things we don't need, encourage people to eat unhealthy food, or are annoying.

Love it or hate it, marketing is part of our society. But that doesn't mean we have to simply accept ads and other sales pitches at face value. It's important for all of us to question marketing messages, to ask ourselves what we really need to be happy or cool or have more fun, and if buying something is going to get us there.

Talk about playing with your emotions. Researchers have found that the more kids are involved in consumer culture—marketing through TV, print, the Internet, apps, etc.—the more likely they will suffer from depression and anxiety, and feel badly about themselves.

Many advertisers rely on old-fashioned views of boys and girls to sell products. Boys are often presented as liking sports, doing math, and building stuff, while girls supposedly only want to play with dolls, paint their nails, and dress up like princesses. But these are stereotypes that send false messages to kids that they should act that way. It makes it seem as if those are the only choices for boys or girls.

It's in the Can

Have you ever noticed one of the characters in your favorite movie, TV show, or video game drinking a brand name soft drink? It seems natural because that's what lots of people do in regular life. But it's no fluke—it's likely a deliberate advertisement placed by the drink company. The actor or the people who made the movie or game are paid to drink that brand and look like they are enjoying it!

It's called product placement and it's one way marketers promote their food or drink without appearing to be selling you something. They've had to get smarter about how they market their products, in part because new technologies allow people to skip the ads they don't want to watch.

Product placement works because simply seeing a brand over and over encourages us to feel loyal to it. Also, when a character we like does something that looks fun or even just refreshing, we often want to do it, too. Maybe we hope we'll be more like our favorite character if we eat or drink the product they seem to love. Sometimes product placement is so woven into the storyline, people don't even realize it's an ad.

A recent *Transformers* movie featured product placement from 55 different brands, including numerous products from China. When it was released, the film became the top-grossing movie in Chinese history, and a prime marketing vehicle for Chinese food and drink ranging from milk and liquor to a fast food retailer known for its spicy duck necks.

The city of Philadephia—one of the largest and also poorest in the U.S.A.—passed a groundbreaking new tax on sweetened beverages. Some of the projected $91 million a year this "soda tax" generates will go toward improving parks, community centers and the education system.

As sugary drink sales fall in North America, beverage companies are investing billions of dollars a year in low- and middle-income countries such as Brazil, China, Mexico, and India. But with diabetes and obesity rates soaring, some of these countries are choosing to create new taxes on the drinks. Mexico's 2014 tax on soda resulted in an immediate dip in sales; Chile followed suit with a soda tax in 2015.

A typical 355 mL soft drink contains 32-40 grams of sugar—that's more than the maximum amount of sugar the World Health Organization suggests an average person should consume in an entire day. No wonder people sometimes call it liquid candy!

Product placement appears in lots of digital games. There might be ads on the side of the sports pitch, or characters who come across billboards as they wander a city. In some games, characters can eat chips or drink a brand name soda to restore their health. McDonald's in Japan has developed a sponsorship agreement with the popular mobile app Pokémon Go. Japanese gamers are encouraged to visit real-life locations of the burger chain where they can train or battle their virtual Pokémon characters.

Word of Mouth

There was a time when "going viral" meant you'd come down with a nasty flu virus. Now every marketer who posts something online or on social media hopes to spread the word about their brand like a fast-moving flu bug. "Going viral" is when something—a video, an app, song, photograph, quote—gets seen and shared by many people in a short amount of time.

Fast-food and beverage companies create ads they hope will get people talking about their products—and, of course, buying them! If the ad is funny or clever or touching enough, people will forward it to their friends. This is sometimes called friendvertising because it relies on you to share with people you know to spread the word. You probably don't think of it this way, but when you send the link, you're giving the company free publicity.

Lately, fast-food restaurants have been creating more and more outrageous products—things like pizza cake, waffle tacos, deep-fried mac 'n' cheese bites with a crunchy chip crust, burger burritos—because the wackier the food, the more likely it is that young people will want to share on social media.

Viral marketing of fast food through mobile devices has seen a huge increase in the last few years. In just one year, fast-food restaurants placed six billion ads on Facebook; Taco Bell's YouTube videos were viewed almost 14 million times.

When Domino's opened in Nigeria in 2012, many people weren't familiar with pizza. To attract customers and spread the word, the company offered common Nigerian foods as pizza toppings, including Jollof rice, which is rice mixed with tomatoes and red peppers, and chicken Suya, a spicy skewered chicken.

Have you ever provided personal info (like age or grade) when you sign up for prizes online, or included a friend's email address to get an extra reward? Be careful. That's valuable information! And you don't know how it will be used—your privacy might even be at risk. Companies gather this data to create more ads targeted at you and your friends. They might even sell your private info to another company.

In Italy, people take their pizza very seriously. When McDonald's ran an ad set in an old-style Italian restaurant featuring a little boy telling the waiter he'd prefer a Happy Meal to the traditional pizza pie, the country's top pizza chefs threatened legal action. They claimed the ad was an attack on Italian cultural traditions.

A few years ago, fried chicken chain KFC went viral with a YouTube video in which a boy shows up at a girl's house dressed for prom. He gives her a box and inside, instead of a flower, there's a fried chicken leg to wear around her wrist as a corsage. The girl is surprised but thrilled! During their final slow dance, she leans in toward him and instead of a kiss, she takes a bite out of her fried chicken corsage. The ad, aimed at high schoolers, got 650,000 hits on YouTube in its first week.

Big Talk:
Speaking Out Against Junk Food

When nine-year-old Hannah Robertson began talking at the McDonald's annual meeting in a Chicago suburb, she was nervous. Really, really nervous. But the grade schooler from British Columbia, Canada, sounded calm, cool, and collected when she delivered tough questions about fast-food marketing to the head of the restaurant chain.

"Don't you want kids to be healthy so they can live a long and happy life?" she asked. "It would be nice if you stopped trying to trick kids into wanting to eat your food all the time." She pointed to toys and cartoon mascots as a big part of the problem.

The head of McDonald's took the questions in stride. He told her his company doesn't sell junk food and that his own kids eat the chain's food, as well as fruits and veggies. But Robertson had made her point—and started an important conversation about how kids can make a difference. Media around the world featured her as a kid who stood up to fast-food marketing.

Today, there's a growing movement of parents and kids speaking out against marketing unhealthy food to kids.

Fast Moving Waters: Cracking Down on Kidvertising

On a remote stretch of the Amazon River in Brazil, a large vessel moved along the waterway, its sides plastered with images of chocolate milk and infant formula. This floating supermarket was sponsored by Nestlé, the world's largest food and beverage company, and it carried over 300 products—including ice cream, chocolate, and juices—to people who have little access to large stores.

The mobile grocery was part of a strategy to attract the growing population of Brazilians with money to spend. Brazil has seen nearly 30 million people rise out of poverty since 2003, providing a huge new market for processed foods.

As Brazilians have embraced fast food, the country has also seen a big increase in diet-related illness. Childhood hunger used to be common, now one in three Brazilian kids is overweight.

Parents, teachers, and health care workers blame low cost, widespread availability and lack of information about the health impact of processed foods.

They also point to the reach and power of marketing—even in the most isolated parts of the country.

A few years ago, the children's arm of Brazil's Ministry of Human Rights passed a resolution proposing a ban on all advertising to kids, calling it "abusive" because it encourages unhealthy behavior. But the ban hasn't been instituted yet, and the battle for the hearts and bellies of Brazilians is far from over.

The country's new nutrition guidelines, however, suggest a hopeful future. Hailed all over the world for their forward thinking, these guidelines focus not just on eating whole, unprocessed foods but the importance of environmental sustainability and the pleasure of slowing down and sharing a meal together.

Game Time

In most countries around the world, there are some limits on what advertisers can promote to kids on TV. But the Internet is different. It changes all the time and it's harder to control. Many parents have no idea what their kids are doing online.

Food and drink companies have grabbed this opportunity to promote themselves and created such things as branded filters for popular apps like Snapchat, free interactive games, and websites focused on their products. Such games are called advergames because they look like entertainment but they are really just big ads.

Many of the games follow a familiar platform format: a character goes on an adventure or has to find something to get to the next level. And guess what? Drinking the sports drink or eating the sugar cereal gives the character strength and power. Sometimes gamers can access more features if they go out and buy the product at a store, then input a special code into the game.

Most of these free games highlight food and drinks that are full of sugar, salt, and fat. Marketers keep kids coming back with special offers, clubs to join, and prizes if they get their friends to play. They're effective, too. A study from the University of Connecticut's Rudd Center found that kids playing fast-food advergames ate more unhealthy snacks and fewer fruit and vegetables than kids playing other games.

Plastic bottles like this one are a major source of pollution around the world. In the U.S., only about three of every ten plastic bottles gets recycled. The rest end up in landfill, leaching chemicals into land and waterways as the plastic slowly disintegrates.

Gatorade, the sports drink brand, offered a mobile game in which an animated version of Usain Bolt, the famous sprinter, raced through a series of challenges collecting gold coins. If Bolt drank Gatorade he became supercharged, but he had to avoid the water droplets because they slowed him down. The game was downloaded millions of times, but activists and doctors complained, saying water is actually the best choice for most young athletes. Today the game is no longer available.

Energize Your Day

EnergY drink

KFC is the biggest fast-food chain in China. In one hugely successful social media campaign, teenagers and young adults who bought a special meal received not only a small figurine of members of popular Korean/Chinese boy band EXO but access to a mobile advergame, a platform to share selfies, a daily cartoon, and many other KFC and EXO tie-ins. Within one month, kids had logged 33 years worth of playing time.

1.2 million American kids from six to eleven years old visit advergame sites every month and spend more than an hour playing the games each time.

In Doughnuts We Trust

Imagine your teacher dressed up in a fast-food uniform standing behind a restaurant counter flipping burgers. Would you go with your family to cheer them on, maybe have some French fries and a soft drink? What if part of the money from your meal went to your school? Sound like a win-win situation? At McTeacher's Night at McDonald's across the U.S.A., teachers, principals—even students—work the grill and raise money for sports' uniforms, trips, or extracurriculars.

And McDonald's isn't the only food company sponsoring school fundraising events. Hershey's offers up its candy bars, Krispy Kreme provides doughnuts, and other companies supply reduced-cost cookie dough to schools to help raise money for cash-strapped classrooms.

But researchers at the Rudd Center have shown these branded fundraisers don't raise much money for most participating schools. They also end up undermining teachers and parents who are trying to encourage healthy eating. Turns out the winners are the fast-food companies who use this cheap marketing tool to reach kids where they are every day: school. The programs build loyalty to the brands, and because the fundraiser is connected to teachers and schools, it seems as if these unhealthy foods are getting a thumbs up from the education system.

CHOCOLATE

Almost two-thirds of all American elementary schools hand out coupons from fast-food restaurants such as Pizza Hut as a reward for good grades or reading a certain number of books.

Food and drink companies spend nearly $150 million a year advertising to kids inside American schools. Until recently, 93 percent of it was for sugary pop and other beverages. But new federal rules now ban marketing unhealthy foods and beverages in public schools.

Most people think of doughnuts as a rare, sweet treat. But a single can of pop—something many drink every day—has about three times more sugar!

One school-based fundraiser encourages families to buy specially marked General Mills' products—including lots of snack cakes and sugar cereals—and clip the labels. The kids bring the labels or "box tops" to school and redeem them through the company at ten cents per label. But the rewards are generally small—you'd have to buy about fifty boxes of sugary cereal to earn a five dollar contribution to your school.

Out of Line:
Standing Up for Junk Free Checkouts

Have you ever noticed how chocolates, sweets, chips, and gum are placed near the checkout line in your local grocery store? Well, it's no accident. Grocery stores are carefully designed to encourage you to buy more stuff. All that junk by the checkout is meant to increase impulse purchases—buying on the spur of the moment when you're bored or just waiting to be served.

Nearly ninety percent of the checkout foods aren't healthy, according to researchers in Sheffield, England. And many of them are placed at exactly the right height to get kids' interest.

For several years, British parents, with the help of the nonprofit food organization, Sustain, and the British Dietetic Association, have been trying to make the case that it isn't fair for stores to tempt kids with junk foods. After all, diet-related illnesses like diabetes and obesity are big problems in Britain, as they are elsewhere around the world, and eating too many of these foods isn't healthy for anyone.

So they created a campaign called Junk Free Checkouts that encourages customers to give pass or fail report cards to their local stores. Fail for those who stock unhealthy snacks by the cash, pass for those who do not. Junk Free got a boost when two of the biggest grocery stores in the country, Tesco and Lidl, opted to only offer good-for-you snacks at their checkouts. Several other chains have since followed suit.

Dear Store Manager,
Thank you for making it easier for me to make healthy eating choices for my family. Please continue to keep unhealthy food and drink products away from all your checkouts and queuing areas in this store, replacing them with healthy alternatives and/ or non-food products. I would like to see this adopted as a company-wide policy, implemented across all stores.
www.junkfreecheckouts.org

Children's Food Campaign

THE BRITISH DIETETIC ASSOCIATION

P

Your store has passed the **checkout test**
Thank you for not placing or promoting unhealthy snacks by the checkouts

F

Your store has failed the **checkout test**
Please stop placing or promoting unhealthy snacks by the checkouts

Dear Store Manager,
You are making it harder for me to make healthy eating choices for my family. Please permanently remove unhealthy food and drink products from all your checkouts and queuing areas in this store and replace them with healthy alternatives and / or non-food products. I would like to see this adopted as a company-wide policy, implemented across all stores.
www.junkfreecheckouts.org

Children's Food Campaign

THE BRITISH DIETETIC ASSOCIATION

Fruit, Glorious Fruit: Playing With Your Food

Most of the food ads we see are for salty snacks, fast food, and soft drinks. But one grocery store chain in France is trying to change that. The ad is simple: a shiny green apple glistening with water droplets on a bright white background.

Only this apple is different. Really different. It has an enormous tumor-like growth coming out of the top. "A grotesque apple . . . a day keeps the doctor away as well," the ad announces.

Other images in Intermarché's cheeky marketing campaign promote the ugly carrot (with two thick roots but still great in soup), the ridiculous potato (perfect for mashing though it has bumps and nobs) and the hideous orange (delicious in juice despite a massive navel).

Many grocery stores won't accept such produce from farmers, because they believe customers won't buy it. As a result, lots of odd-looking but perfectly good food is just thrown away. Every year, about 88 million tonnes of food goes to waste in the European Union.

But shoppers at Intermarché didn't mind the ugly produce after all—especially offered at a thirty percent discount. Buzz from the funny ads attracted new customers, who also tried juices and soups made from the fruit and veg. Intermarché sold 1.2 tonnes of the produce per store over the first two days of the campaign!

The ad's success has prompted other grocers to do the same. Watch for strange but lovable fruits and veggies coming soon to a store near you!

What a Character

When kids are as young as two or three years old, many already know the familiar mascots connected to fast-food and drink brands. Some recognize popular spokescharacters before knowing their own name! All over the world, characters like Burger King, Ronald McDonald, and Tony the Tiger act as colorful representatives of their brand. It's a kind of marketing that works especially well with kids because the characters are designed to be friendly and fun. Children know them and trust them.

In a study published in an American medical journal, kids were offered the same food—one with, the other without a familiar character on the package. More than half the kids told researchers the product connected to the spokescharacter tasted better—even though it was exactly the same!

And this loyalty lasts a really long time. Adults who knew and loved a particular fast-food character when they were young often still feel strongly about them as grownups—even though they probably know the food isn't healthy.

MOM's Organic Market, a small American grocery chain, doesn't carry any product using spokescharacters aimed at kids. Even though the product might be organic and healthy, the company founder believes marketing to children is unfair and should be against the law.

Health concerns have caused North American sales of processed foods like breakfast cereal to shrink in recent years. But African nations such as Kenya and Nigeria are the new frontier for packaged foods and snacks. Kellogg, maker of such popular sugary cereals as Froot Loops, recently invested hundreds of millions in a West African company to expand its presence in that growing market.

Ireland has banned celebrities and sports stars from promoting fast foods to children on TV and radio. Now, the Irish Heart Foundation is calling for regulation of digital media, including Facebook, where fast-food and beverage brands actively recruit users to spread their message.

Breakfast cereals are some of the most heavily marketed food products. Companies spent about $264 million a year to advertise cereal to kids—and most of it is the sugary kind.

According to Cornell University researchers, the mascots on sugar cereal boxes are trying to make eye contact with you! Research suggests the boxes' placement and height on grocery store shelves means the characters gain kids' trust and affection by looking them in the eye. Cereal producer General Mills denies the findings, calling the claims "absurd."

Advertisers know kids look up to famous athletes. That's why they've hired superstars like LeBron James and Peyton Manning to promote their products. But nearly 80 percent of the food products and 93 percent of the beverages athletes endorse aren't good for you—or for pro athletes! NBA All-Star Stephen Curry bucked the trend recently when he agreed to promote Brita water filters, encouraging everyone to drink more H_2O.

Many food and drink companies have their own mascots, but some borrow popular characters from TV or movies to sell their products. Sometimes these "licensed" characters are even used to sell healthy foods. SpongeBob Square Pants and Dora the Explorer have appeared on fresh food like spinach, carrots, and edamame beans—as well as sugary snacks.

Picture Perfect

Most people have heard that the photographs of supermodels and celebrities who appear on billboards and in magazines have been digitally altered to look perfect. But you might not know that advertisers also rework photos of food!

And those pictures of fresh, juicy hamburgers or overstuffed tacos actually make people crave them. Scientists have shown that simply seeing food makes people want to eat—even if they aren't hungry.

But there are often so many alterations to the food before the photo is taken and digital manipulation afterward that what you buy at the store or restaurant doesn't look anything like the pictures. What a lunch bag letdown!

It's a lot of work to make fast-food hamburgers look picture perfect. To get the right bun, food photographers sometimes have to go through bag after bag just to find what they call "the hero." And even then, they might need to glue on tiny sesame seeds for the photos. The hamburger in the image itself probably isn't even cooked all the way through because it would look too dried out. Instead, it's left raw on the inside, and quickly browned outside to appear plump and fresh. Barbecue char marks are sometimes added with a paint brush and shoe polish!

More than 300 million people in India—that's about the population of the entire U.S.A.—are vegetarian. When American fast-food giant Burger King opened its first stores there, it made a splash on social media with half the menu entirely meat-free and no beef or pork at all.

It's not just pictures of food that are altered. Some fast-food companies have laboratories where they create the flavors people crave. By mixing just the right amount of fat, sugar, and salt in each product such companies hope to reach what is known as the "bliss point"—the moment when your mouth tells your brain the food tastes just right, and you want more!

People often complain fast-food hamburgers are smaller in real life than in the ads. But portion sizes for the average fast-food meal today are three times larger than they were in the 1950s.

Next time you eat a fast-food burger, consider its impact on the environment. Producing a double quarter pounder requires 26 ounces of oil —four full glasses worth. And that's just for the meat: the fertilizer and pesticides used to grow the corn or soy the cows eat, as well as the fuel required to transport and process the animals.

Too Good to be True

Over the last decade, people have become more aware of the connection between their health and the food they eat. Food and beverage companies have responded with tons of new products—and advertising promises.

"A great source of calcium/protein/iron."

"All natural!"

Sound familiar?

Even longstanding junk food products have been made to seem healthier. Sugary cereals announce: "Now with whole grains!" on the front of the box. Fast-food restaurants list "Healthier for you" products on their menus. It would be great if it were true, but according to research from the U.S.-based Prevention Institute, more than eighty percent of so-called healthier products offered in stores and restaurants don't meet even basic nutritional standards.

It's confusing and frustrating to sort through all the promises—especially when there's a new study each week with different advice about what we should be eating or not eating.

So who should we believe? Sometimes the simplest advice is the best (if not the easiest to follow). Consider writer Michael Pollan's famous words: "Eat food [meaning real whole foods like vegetables, fruit, and grains]. Not too much. Mostly plants."

A number of years ago a Frosted Mini-Wheats' marketing campaign promoted its cereal as brain food. The ads suggested eating the cereal would help improve kids' ability to focus by nearly twenty percent. But the numbers didn't add up. The American Federal Trade Commission complained and barred the company from making the claim.

In Canada, when you see the word "natural" on a food label, it means the food has never contained an added vitamin, nutrient, flavor, or additive. Food companies can use the term "natural ingredients" when vitamins or minerals are added—so long as they come from natural sources. Remember: just because it's natural, doesn't mean it's good for you!

In Chile, the government has responded to rising rates of obesity, especially among children, with new limits on advertising health claims. Some of the most popular packaged foods now have to include warnings telling families and kids the product is high in fat, sugar, and/or salt.

ALL NATURAL Orange Drink with Vitamin C

When Sunny D was first launched in Britain, the orange drink was marketed as tastier than juice and healthier than soft drinks—though it was only five percent juice plus loads of sugar and additives. It became one of the biggest drink brands in the country. Then word got out that a little girl's skin turned orange and yellow after drinking large quantities every day, and sales tanked.

With parents worried about their children's diet, there are many new products that get picky kids eating vegetables. Kraft Dinner has a mac 'n' cheese with cauliflower mixed in the sauce; Mott's sells apple sauce with "undercover" veggies. But hiding vegetables in processed food doesn't make a product healthy— they're often still packed with salt or sugar. And what message does it send about healthy food when adults have to trick kids into eating it?

Food labels in Sweden don't just include ingredients and health promises, some also show the product's impact on the planet. These labels calculate the environmental cost associated with producing the item and encourage people to eat whole foods that don't require as much energy to grow or make.

A Sticky Wicket:
Tackling Unhealthy Advertising in Sports

When Australian dad Aaron Schultz first got his two young boys a cricket set, he was excited to share his love of the sport. But when they sat down together to watch professional matches on TV, Schultz was shocked.

Advertisements for unhealthy fast food, gambling, and alcohol were everywhere from the grass to the grandstands to players' shirts. And that's not even including the TV commercials shown at breaks.

Schultz remembered the powerful impact cigarette ads associated with his sports heroes had on him when he was young and began smoking. He started to worry that promoting junk food and alcohol through athletics would encourage his kids to indulge in unhealthy activities. So he created an online petition calling on cricket and other sports organizations to stop promoting unhealthy products.

Schultz quickly won support from parents and some Australian health organizations. His campaign, called Game Changer, also received lots of media attention when he created massive billboards—just like the ones pushing junk food—and put them up

during a key cricket competition. Over a photo of a young boy holding a beer and a massive, greasy hamburger, the billboard blared What is Cricket Australia selling your family?

Schultz has now turned his attention to rugby and Australian rules football. His goal: nothing less than getting junk food, alcohol, and gambling ads out of sports altogether.

No More Clowning Around:
Cutting Spokescharacters Out of the Picture

For decades, Ronald McDonald, the red-headed mascot behind the Golden Arches hamburger empire, was nearly as well-known as Santa Claus. Launched in the 1960s as a marketing tool aimed at kids, the yellow and red jumpsuit–wearing clown made McDonald's appear fun and friendly. Ronald was featured in TV ads, billboards, video games, even an animated movie series.

But a few years ago, a band of health care professionals, parents, and activists came together to urge Ronald to retire. They argued that such mascots take advantage of kids' trust and undermine parents' efforts to encourage children to eat healthy food.

The Retire Ronald campaign held pretend retirement parties, created petitions, told supporters to send "Best wishes on your retirement" cards to the clown, and called on all fast-food companies to stop using mascots to push unhealthy food and drinks on children.

But McDonald's said Ronald wasn't about to hang up his wig. The company has even introduced a new, modern outfit for the middle-aged mascot.

Yet, Ronald has become less visible in the burger giant's marketing these days. Some say McDonald's itself is having an identity crisis. With greater competition for customers, and people becoming more health conscious, the company is working hard to maintain its share of the market.

Captive Audience

Most people think students should be free to focus on learning at school—not buying stuff. But food and drink companies have found ways to spread their message to kids in schools all over the world. Sometimes it's obvious, like fundraising or fast-food ads plastered on school buses, brand name pizza and hamburgers in cafeterias, or vending machines sponsored by soft drink companies.

But there are also less obvious approaches used in some schools, such as speakers or video content sponsored by fast-food brands. Many international food and beverage companies also create teaching resources—lesson plans, books, handouts, visual aids, and more—on subjects ranging from math and poetry to healthy living. Some schools accept them because they are free, though the company logo, message, and even mascot might appear on the materials.

One British sugary drink company created curriculum resources urging teachers in more than a thousand schools to have their students write poems celebrating the sweet drink. Talk about *creative* writing!

When Japan introduced mandatory food education to try to improve kids' diets, companies jumped at the chance to create lesson plans and go into classes to teach. One chewing gum company offered a lesson on the importance of chewing your food properly, while a soya sauce company provided a teaching resource about the salty sauce.

The Oreo Cookie Counting Book is presented as an educational book—it's also a great big ad for the brand. The book teaches young children to count to ten using colorful pictures of cookies being nibbled, dunked in milk, twisted, stacked, and shared. The toddlers are learning as much about Oreos—and developing loyalty to the cookie—as math skills.

In Peru, where twenty percent of young people and nearly half of adults are overweight, junk food is banned in schools altogether.

For some kids in the Philippines, fast food isn't just in school, it is school. Every summer for more than two decades, McDonald's has run a five-day camp called Kiddie Crew Workshop. Parents pay a fee for their elementary school children to train behind the counter at McDonald's, as well as do dance classes and learn teamwork and discipline.

Pester Power

It might not always seem like it, but kids have a lot of influence on what their parents buy. Some marketing experts estimate that kids' worldwide buying power, including encouraging their parents' purchases, amount to more than a trillion dollars a year!

Those chicken nuggets in the shape of dinosaurs, cheese products you can play with, and yogurt in a tube are all designed so kids will bug their parents to buy them. Advertisers sometimes call this "pester power" because children nag parents or threaten a meltdown if they don't let them have the food or drink.

Offering toys alongside a meal is one of the main ways fast-food restaurants encourage kids to pester their parents to visit. The big chains spend nearly sixty percent of their marketing budgets on toys, games, and puzzles. Colorful play structures and ball rooms also tempt kids in the doors.

But some places, such as Chile and the city of San Francisco, California, have decided it's not fair to encourage young children to eat junk food by offering them toys. They've created legislation banning restaurants from offering free stuff when you buy a meal.

The Walt Disney Company hasn't allowed some of its characters—like Mickey Mouse and Buzz Lightyear—to be used in toy giveaways associated with unhealthy food since 2006. Yet other Disney-related characters continue to be featured on sugar cereal boxes and other kid-focused products.

Under pressure from parents and regulators, many fast-food restaurants in the U.S. are trying to make kids' meals healthier. But researchers have found that while most of the meals targeted at children are within the recommended range for calories, they're still high in salt and fat.

Toy Inside

Kiddie Meal

Tayto, a large potato chip company in Ireland, has its very own theme park to promote its brand to kids. At Tayto Park near Dublin there are potato-themed attractions, a tour of the factory, and, of course, a top-hat–wearing potato mascot named Mr. Tayto.

Packaging from fast-food restaurants often includes toys, boxes, paper, napkins, drinks, straws, foil, and bags. It's one of the largest sources of litter on the streets of England.

Toys get kids in the door, but some fast-food restaurants have also created targeted websites, TV, and web-based banner ads aimed at African-American and Hispanic children and teens. This kind of focused marketing is on the increase. Already black children and teens in the U.S. see about sixty percent more ads for fast food than white youth.

A Message to Students, Parents, and Teachers

Fast food and drinks have become part of our shared global culture. Everywhere we go around the world, we see similar brands, products, logos, and mascots.

This book is a guide to recognizing and understanding the techniques and strategies marketers use to promote these foods and drinks to kids. But it's also about the way such products affect many things we all care about, like our health—both our bodies and our minds—our communities, and the planet we share.

When we begin to see the connections between marketing and these important parts of our lives, we have to ask some tough questions. Are the products we are being sold and many of us are eating and drinking regularly actually good for us or good for the environment? We have to ask, too, if the marketing strategies are simply fun and entertaining, or if misinformation, harmful stereotypes, and manipulation are being used to sell us unhealthy stuff.

Who's responsible?

In response to these issues raised by parents, kids, and children's advocates, food and beverage corporations in some countries, such as the U.S. and Canada, have created their own guidelines that limit the kinds of marketing aimed at kids. But in many cases, these self-imposed regulations are too weak, or aren't respected, and there aren't real consequences for companies that fail to adapt. Plus, such rules don't always keep pace with the many new technologies and media platforms being created.

Parents, of course, have an important role to play in limiting their children's exposure to harmful messages and helping them make healthy choices about what they eat. They can also support their kids to decode the marketing they see and experience.

Some people, in fact, say it is entirely up to parents to limit the fast food made available to their children. But it's clear that parents alone are no match for marketers all over the world who spend billions of dollars pushing cheap, easily available fast food and beverages on kids through toys, games, songs, billboards, books, TV, movies, apps, celebrity promoters, and mascots. Some of the marketers even undermine parental authority with ads that make fun of adult rules or suggest parents just don't understand their kids.

And the marketing works. Sales explode following a successful viral campaign, kids choose branded food over the exact same item without the brand or spokescharacter. Marketers wouldn't spend all that money if it wasn't effective. For parents trying the best they can for their children, it's simply not a level playing field.

Governments act

That's why governments in many nations and cities are starting to take positions in this debate. Research has revealed that the brains of children under the age of eight aren't developed enough to tell the difference between paid marketing and other types of information. They need the help of adults who have their health and welfare top of mind to protect them. In places such as Chile, Peru, Mexico, Sweden, the Netherlands, Norway, the U.K., and the Canadian province of Quebec, governments have created laws and regulations to do just that, limiting kids' exposure to marketing that promotes unhealthy food and drinks. The rules aren't always as effective as some would like, but these governments understand that the consequences of doing nothing are serious—including long-term health problems, damage to the environment, and the creation of a society of consumers rather than engaged citizens.

Of course, kids can help push for legislation and also arm themselves with the tools to make sense of marketing when they see it. With information and skills, children can begin to interpret the messages they see and grasp how it's affecting them. They can ask good questions about whether marketing is promoting products in their best interest or if they're full of hot air. Children can also speak up and tell companies that they're not going to eat fast food and drink sugary beverages that make them sick. Kids have the power to take charge of what they eat and fight to change the food system.

DO*THIS*!

Now that you've read this book, you can use your skills to recognize and understand fast-food and beverage marketing out in the world. But there are also other hands-on (and delicious!) ways you can challenge fast-food culture in your daily life.

People everywhere are beginning to understand that part of the reason it's so easy to convince us with marketing schemes promising ease, convenience, and happiness-in-a-box, is that we've become disconnected from where our food comes from. Many of us have no idea how the food we eat gets from field to table. Lots of kids don't even realize that beans grow on vines or potatoes grow in the ground!

But like Hannah Robertson, who spoke out against fast-food marketing, we can all reclaim our food, our health, and the well-being of our planet— starting at home and school. Plant a school food garden; learn cooking skills to make yummy, healthy food for yourself and your family; write to stores and food companies and ask them to offer food that's delicious and good for you; push for access to healthy, sustainable food for everyone.

Here are some other ways you can get involved in challenging fast-food culture and marketing strategies.

Celebrate diversity: Host a potluck with homemade dishes. Ask people with different cultural backgrounds to bring their special recipes and tell others about them. Make your own school or class cookbook.

Choose your own adventure: Advocate for a delicious, fresh salad bar with lots of interesting ingredients as part of your school lunch. Research how it might work in your school. Are there special programs or grants to help buy materials like a fridge or sink? Can you buy the ingredients from local farmers or at a nearby market?

Price check: Do a taste test comparing a meal from a fast-food restaurant and a similar one you make yourself. Which one is more delicious, more expensive, more healthy? Which creates the least amount of waste?

Garbage delight: Do a litter audit at your school. Can you reduce the amount of garbage by creating a litterless lunch campaign?

Advocate: Write letters to your principal, school board, parent council, and local politicians demanding your school become a fast-food marketing-free zone.

Question media. Ask why a particular ad was made. What is it selling? Why is it appearing at this moment or in a particular location? How does the ad make you feel?

Watch your favorite show or play your favorite video game with a scorecard beside you. Mark down how many times you see product placement. If you're with a friend, make it a game to see who spots the most. Are the products targeted at a certain kind of person? Are you the target?

Think about the videos, quotes, or photos that have gone viral. Are there common themes? What are the necessary elements for something to capture people's attention? Could you make an ad focused on healthy food that everyone wants to share?

Read the nutrition label on your cereal box. Did you know ingredients are listed in order of their quantity? If sugar is the first or second item in the ingredients' list it means there's a lot of sugar in the cereal! (Remember: sugar goes by lots of different names, including cane juice, corn sweetener, dextran, diatase, ethyl maltol, fructose, and glucose!)

Does your school do a food-based fundraiser? Is the food healthy? How much money has your school made from the fundraiser (don't forget to put a price to all the volunteer labor). Compare this to the amount the company receives. Are there other benefits to the company (for instance, loyalty to their brand)?

Quick: think of all the fast-food mascots you know by name. Write them down on a piece of paper. Make it a contest with your friends. How many are selling healthy food? Which creatures are the most common—birds, animals, monsters, or humans? Who are the mascots aimed at?

You read about the Retire Ronald campaign on page 27. Can you think of other fast-food spokescharacters who should retire? Write a persuasive letter and explain why they should stop marketing to kids.

Walk around your school and make a list of all the food and beverage marketing you see. What are the most common brands? Are there any healthy food products advertised in your school? Do the same thing in your neighborhood. Create a map and highlight all the marketing you see. How much of it is targeted at children?

Glossary

Activist: a person who works actively to create change in their community and/or the world

Additive: something added to food to change it; for example, to make it sweeter

Brand: a particular make of a product, as in a *brand of pop*

Commercial: noun: a television or radio advertisement; adjective: having money-making as the primary aim, as in *a commercial venture*

Consumer: someone who buys and uses products or services

Diabetes: a disease characterized by too much sugar (glucose) in the blood

Diet-related illness: sickness resulting from what a person eats or drinks on a regular basis, including obesity and certain kinds of diabetes and cancers

Digital: of, or relating to, electronic form; readable, usable on a computer

Logo: a symbol or grouping of images that represent a particular company, organization, or brand

Manipulate: to influence people to do what you want them to do

Mineral: naturally occurring ingredients found in food that are essential to the functioning of the human body, as in calcium, iron or sodium

Nutrient: an element inside food that people need to eat to stay healthy, such as protein, minerals, and vitamins

Obesity: the medical condition of being very overweight

Petition: a letter signed by many people aimed at governments or corporations, asking for changes in policies or actions on a certain issue

Platform game: a kind of computer game played by moving a figure on the screen through a series of obstacles

Portion size: the amount of food served to someone, as determined by the restaurant or person serving it

Protein: a necessary nutrient required by the body for growth, repair, and maintenance of all cells

Spokescharacter: a character, often a cartoon, who speaks on behalf of a brand

Strategy: a detailed and carefully thought-out plan for achieving a particular goal

Targeted ads: advertisements that are aimed at a specific individual or group

Technique: a specific method, or way of completing a task, that is carefully considered in order to achieve one's goal

Whole foods: foods that have not been processed or refined and have no additives. Fresh vegetables and many grains are examples of whole foods

A Note on Sources

Many different sources were used to research this book. Whenever possible, the most recent statistics have been used. The following resources can be used to support further learning.

Berkeley Media Studies Group produces research on media literacy (www.bmsg.org).

Bettina Elias Siegel's blog, The Lunch Tray, is focused on kids and food (www.thelunchtray.com).

Center for Science in the Public Interest has developed many resources on health, nutrition, and marketing to children (cspinet.org).

Corporate Accountability International campaigns on many issues, including against marketing to children (www.stopcorporateabuse.org).

DigitalAds: Exposing How Marketers Target Youth (www.digitalads.org).

Food Myth Busters is a source of information, films, and great ideas (www.foodmyths.org).

Healthy Eating Research: Building Evidence to Prevent Childhood Obesity (www.healthyeatingresearch.org).

MediaSmarts produces fact sheets, parental information, and curriculum resources on fast-food marketing and consumerism (www.mediasmarts.ca).

Michele Simon is a public health lawyer who writes about food (www.eatdrinkpolitics.com).

Prevention Institute is behind "We're Not Buying It," focused on stopping junk food marketing to kids (www.preventioninstitute.org).

Stop Marketing to Kids Coalition is a collaboration between the Canadian Heart & Stroke Foundation and the Childhood Obesity Foundation (www.stopmarketingtokids.ca).

Sustain: The Alliance for Better Food and Farming (www.sustainweb.org).

The Rudd Center for Food Policy & Obesity at the University of Connecticut (www.uconnruddcenter.org).

Interview with Andrea Curtis

Why did you write this book?

When my oldest son was in kindergarten, the class did an art and literacy project involving brands, largely for fast food and drinks. I was blown away by how many logos, songs, and advertisements these little kids knew, though most of them couldn't even read. But it was going into schools and talking to children about my first book, *What's for Lunch? How Schoolchildren Eat Around the World*, that made me think hard about how pervasive, effective—and potentially damaging—this marketing can be.

Have you ever been persuaded by marketing strategies?

Of course. As I write in the book, marketing works. When I was a teenager, I drank a lot of diet soda. It was a relatively new product at the time, and I was convinced by all the TV and magazine ads featuring happy, sassy girls dancing around that it was my kind of drink. Today I can't even look at a diet soda. I don't touch the stuff anymore.

So what do you tell a kid who says, "I know junk food is bad but it tastes so good."

I know that kid. He lives in my house. My youngest son loves pretty much anything sweet. I encourage him to limit the amount of sugar he consumes when he's out in the world. And we avoid processed food with added sugar at home. But I know lots of people like the taste of certain kinds of fast food and sugary drinks. They're widely available, relatively cheap, people are attached to them (because of marketing), plus the food is engineered to be addictive. So I would say that we all have to ask ourselves if buying into this marketing and taste engineering makes us dupes—doing something that's not in our best interest. But, mostly, I think we have to find the balance that works in our lives—in this case between what tastes good and what's good for us.

Are there other ways you encourage your children to avoid junk food and drinks?

We try not to have that kind of food in our cupboards. If it's not available, you don't eat it. We're lucky to live in a place where it's not hard to find delicious whole foods—from local producers and at farmers' markets. We even grow our own food in a tiny veggie patch. We talk a lot in our family about food and how it's grown, made, distributed, packaged, marketed, etc. I think education is a really big part of this story—both in school and at home.

What else do you do to push back against such marketing?
Well, I wrote this book. And I hope it gives kids the tools they need to question it themselves.
I also speak at schools and to community groups about changing the food system. And I am working with many others to encourage politicians and lawmakers here in Canada to create protections from marketing for children. I'm really encouraged by recent momentum on this issue as more and more kids, parents, and educators see the negative impact of fast-food culture.

On the personal front, I've spent many years volunteering with a local school to build a large edible garden where children get their hands dirty learning how to grow fresh, organic foods. I love seeing the kids take such pride in their efforts, and watching them discover they actually love green things like kale and basil. By eating the food they grow themselves they are actively retraining their brains and tastebuds. I think school gardens can be one important part of challenging fast-food culture.

Why do you think working on food issues is so important?
It's no news to anyone that we have to eat every day—ideally several times a day. But food isn't simply fuel for our bodies and minds. It's at the heart of so many of the issues I care deeply about: health, community, and the environment. What we eat affects nearly every part of our lives and the life of our planet. I believe that if we can build a more just and healthy food system we can forge a better world for everyone.

You write books for both children and adults. Which is harder? Why?
Writing any book is hard and takes a long time, but writing books for kids is definitely harder. Children's books might be shorter but they also have to be concise and clear. There's no room for extra words, and I edit over and over (and over) to try to make the writing as tight and straightforward and interesting as possible.

Thank you, Andrea.